A Quiet Walk on the Beach

A Quiet Walk
on the Beach

EXPLORING THE BEAUTY OF AMERICA'S SEASHORE

Written and Photographed by
FREDRIC WINKOWSKI

SILVER LINING BOOKS
New York

Produced and designed by Fredric Winkowski

For information address:
Silver Lining Books, 122 Fifth Avenue, New York, NY 10011

Library of Congress Cataloging-in-Publication Data is available on request.

ISBN 0-7607-3163-2

Printed in Singapore

987654321

First Edition

This book is dedicated to my family, which has been my companion on many beach adventures. It is especially dedicated to my wife, Sally, who is always first to reach the beach and last to leave.

Acknowledgments

Thanks to the rangers, employees, and volunteers of the national parks, seashores, and national wildlife refuges, whose assistance and information put this very big subject in perspective for me.

Introduction

I love the beach. It is a place of great beauty and inspiration for me, but I must admit that was not always so. Once, it seemed to me that the glare of the sun, the hot sand, and the crowds of a noontime beach were more torture than pleasure.

But I've since discovered another beach, a beach of glorious sunrises and thrilling sunsets, the cool delicious beach of springtime and autumn, the quiet isolated beach that brings closeness to nature, and the expansive beach where we most certainly witness the heavens meet the earth. That is my beach, the beach I eventually found and now treasure. And I think that is really the beach that many people also love and dream about.

There is so much that is sensuous about the beach. There is the tangy smell of the ocean, the fragrance of a tropical forest, and the sight of great flocks of snow geese wheeling overhead. And the web of

vegetation, the sea grass, and the salt marshes that hold the fragile coastal lands together.

This book is part guide, part inspiration, and partly an invitation to come out and enjoy our country's treasured seashore. I've chosen some of the loca-tions here because they are places I know and love. Other places are spots I longed to visit but never before had. As far as I'm concerned, they are all wonderful.

In the end, a quiet walk on the beach is a very per-sonal, even spiritual experience. On very special days, when the sun is striking the beach at a certain magical angle, I find that the world truly seems touched with glory. I hope that your quiet walks on the beach bring you days like that too.

Sanibel Island

Lush subtropical Sanibel Island is known for magnificent sunsets, some of the best beaches in the world for collecting seashells, and a large wildlife refuge that is home to countless aquatic birds. The community of Sanibel has a strong sense of natural preservation, and half of the island is devoted to wildlife refuges. The other half, though definitely commercial, shows a welcome civilized restraint. Sanibel and its neighboring island, Captiva, sit just off Fort Myers, Florida, on the Gulf coast.

Memory of a tree reaches even now into the clouds.

The beaches of Sanibel Island have a casual but cultivated personality. The days are warm, the breezes gentle, the clouds soft and fluffy, and the surf mild and hypnotic. The shell-covered beaches are firm and wide and perfect for a long stroll.

The gentle beaches of the Gulf coast are a real contrast to the dramatic, surf-pounded beaches on the Atlantic Ocean. Some would think it romantic to face the sea spray on the Atlantic. On the other hand, a Gulf beach might be thought of as a refuge; mild, undemanding, and welcoming.

searchlights and shells

*Bright circle
of light, sleeping
beside the trees.*

This imposing ironwork lighthouse is a landmark on Sanibel's east-end beach. Built in 1884, the beacon was originally fueled by kerosene. The lighthouse is still in service but with an updated electric light. Just beyond the lighthouse is the island's fishing pier, and beyond that is the long causeway connecting Sanibel with the mainland.

Bowman Beach on the west side of the island has especially impressive dunes of seashells. Most barrier islands tend to be oriented in a north–south direction. Sanibel, however, thrusts into the Gulf of Mexico at a forty-five-degree angle and efficiently snags seashells in the incoming surf. Young and old can be seen carrying shell buckets, but dedicated collectors carry flashlights and scour the beach before sunrise.

Sanibel's J. N. "Ding" Darling National
Wildlife Refuge is host to more than two hundred
species of birds. This anhinga, which spears fish
with its pointed beak, dries its wings atop a mangrove tree.

A two-mile-long footpath, the Indigo Trail, ends
near the refuge's Wildlife Drive. Nearby, an alli-
gator sleeps peacefully, one would hope, after a
large and satisfying meal.

The curve-billed white ibis feeds at low tide in the mudflats, among the mangrove trees.

Near the Wildlife Drive, a single roseate spoonbill wades through the shallow waters. Late in the winter, great flocks of spoonbills descend at dusk.

solemn beauty

Tall bird watching.
Wondering as the
day disappears.

This great blue heron
was spotted ruling the
beach at Blind Pass, where
Sanibel and Captiva
islands come closest
together. The gorgeous
and fearsome bird had
spent the previous hour
astride this sandy rise, and
clearly he did not intend
to move. The few people
who were taking a sunset
walk on the beach avoided
venturing too close, not
daring to intrude upon
such ferocious beauty.
More than an hour later,
the heron was still there,
absorbing the final min-
utes of daylight.

city of light

*Two birds
live beneath the bridge.
A perfect pair.*

The entire world is touched with glory at sunset. But sometimes the walker on the beach is most rewarded by turning his back on the sun and looking the other way. Things that have spent all day lurking in shadows are now spotlighted as the sun goes down.

Often it is only the overlooked things that have been left undisturbed and remain the most natural. The most humble places, like under a highway overpass, when conditions are right, reveal an unexpected aspect of themselves; concrete blocks transformed into a city of light.

The great egret lurking beneath the bridge at Blind Pass patrols the shallow waters. It is a detail on the beach, but it illuminates that particular moment.

wedding at twilight

White ripples
in the sky.
After all, maybe
it was not the egret.

While quietly appreciating the approaching sunset, I saw a bus filled with merrymakers pulling into the parking lot. It carried a dozen or so guests, arriving for a sunset wedding ceremony on the beach. As the party arranged itself near the water, the location seemed to me an inspired choice for any rite of passage.

Though I soon had to leave, I could imagine some of the words the minister might be saying in such a magnificent setting. How could he not compare the infinite expanse surrounding the bride and groom to the infinite possibilities their new life together would bring? And wasn't the beauty and happiness experienced on a pleasant beach similar to the bliss of two loving souls united?

After the rain,
distant clouds. Here
the sunshine makes a new
path to the beach.

Because Sanibel is in the tropics, or near to them, weather can be uncertain. On a perfect sunny afternoon at the beach, a patch of gray on the horizon can turn into a torrential downpour in a moment. But life on the Gulf Coast is so easy that a sudden storm adds some unforeseen perspective. Rain is always just over the horizon, and you can't avoid it, but it's really like a dark frame surrounding a brilliant painting; it makes everything hang together.

In the time it took to write the few lines above, a sudden squall came and went. People ran, and my notebook got a little wet. Soon shorebirds were again pulling worms from the wet sands and sunlight flooded a sandy path leading to the beach.

the time for beauty

Sanibel is famous for its sunsets. As the sun decends toward the horizon, people hurry to Sanibel's beaches. Recently empty parking lots fill with cars, and beachside residents rush down to the water. This is the great event of the day. A sunset on Sanibel is like a gorgeous exclamation point in the sky proclaiming an end to the activities of the day. All those who gather on the beach witness and honor that wonderful yet somehow solemn moment.

Beauty happens naturally as the unobstructed sun descends over water. When the intensity of the sunlight is right and the ocean's humidity produces a glow in the sky, when colors combine properly, and when shapes and proportions interact to simplify and add sensibility to the chaotic world around, then a moment of beauty occurs, and it is a beauty that is transcendent.

A beautiful sunset is found not just in the sky. People on the beach are also part of the spectacle; so is the sea and everything around. All the world is embraced in the glow. And unlike any other time, we stand on the beach at sunset, attentive to both our own day and the rhythm of the universe.

Assateague Island

Assateague Island is a forty-mile-long barrier island just off the Maryland shore. With a national seashore in the north and a national wildlife refuge in the south, Assateague glows with the pristine character of a historic natural beauty spot. The island is well known for the bands of wild ponies that have roamed free there for hundreds of years.

*Cool night
with many stars.
How can it
be morning now?*

One day in November, in Ocean City, Maryland, I found myself awake at six a.m. Standing on my hotel room's balcony, I gazed with delight at a narrow sliver of the horizon saturated with an uncanny deep rose color. Far above, brilliant stars twinkled in the blackness. It was as much nighttime as it was morning, and the world was asleep. With the light still dim, it was all so smooth, the ocean, the beach—everything. The softly modulated colors were slowly becoming pink and purple. It was as if no details had yet been added to the earth. Only the first broad brushstrokes had been applied to the day.

*My companions
beckon to me,
the seagulls and the sky.*

When I looked up again, I was surprised to see that the top of the sun was now visible above the horizon. Still standing on my hotel balcony, I felt the orange disk of the sun shining its warmth on me. True dawn had come. The sun steadily and perceptibly inched upward, escaping the night . . . and began creating the new day.

I decided to take an early walk on the beach. At first the rows of seagulls facing the wind were my only companions on the beach. Later I walked on the boardwalk, which stretched for miles and ended at the Ocean City amusement pier. Soon other early risers appeared, also enjoying a glorious brisk morning walk or ride.

Still it is summer though snows pile up upon my windowsill.

A day at the beach brings such pleasure that it seems a kind of paradise, a Garden of Eden minus the trees and flowers. Most of the time, swimming, relaxing, and building sand castles at the water's edge are what the beach is all about. But there is obviously more to it.

As an Atlantic barrier island, Assateague is in a state of constant evolution. The ocean deposits sand at one end of the island and removes it from other spots along the beach. This has been going on at Assateague for at least six thousand years. That's really not too long after the end of the last Ice Age. In fact, the melting of the glaciers raised the level of the oceans, making conditions right for the deposit of glacier-generated sand along the relatively shallow Atlantic coast. This is the process that created Assateague and all the other barrier islands.

What holds Assateague and the other islands together is the growth of vegetation, especially the trees, grass, and salt marshes on the mainland-facing side of the islands. Assateague's beach depends on these silent and essential natural partners, its own Garden of Eden, for its continued existence.

*Matchless
is the tower,
enticing the night
with its glory.*

A distant lighthouse is a good destination for a beach walk, but here the beach walked away from the lighthouse. At Chincoteague National Wildlife Refuge (located at the southern end of Assateague Island), shifting sands over the last century have altered the shoreline so that the lighthouse is now a mile inland.

Though inland, today this beacon, with its two one-thousand-watt bulbs,

is still operated by the Coast Guard, and the light can be seen from twenty-two miles away. It alerts ships to the dangerous off-shore shoals.

Unfortunately, ship-wrecks have occurred in nearby waters. The best known was the 1891 wreck of the presidential yacht *Dispatch,* bound for Washington, D.C. There was no loss of life, but the ship was destroyed.

The lighthouse's attractive red-and-white paint job is a modern notion, first applied in 1963.

Smile seagull,
far out at sea.
A new friend
awaits you.

Pounding surf, blowing sand, salt spray in the air, intense summer heat, and punishing winter storms make the barrier island's beaches as inhospitable to life as the desert. Only a few simple creatures—clams, crabs, and insects—claim the beach as their home. Shorebirds such as the sandpiper and plover prowl for those delicacies. It is the surf, that watery cornucopia, that endlessly washes ashore a bounty of organic matter that the gulls depend upon.

Although the osprey and great horned owl are at the top of the flying food chain here, the gull is the major scavenger. It enjoys crabs, clams, bird's eggs, and insects; just about anything is fair game for the gulls of Assateague. However, the gulls themselves are not immune to danger. Gulls are ground-nesting birds, and the island's predators can invade their nests. The red fox, raccoon, and great horned owl are enemies to be reckoned with.

At three in the afternoon, the famous wild ponies of Assateague Island came into view. They seemed to be everywhere; in the dunes, on the roads, and even in the empty parking lots. Though they are wild, the ponies don't fear humans, and they often approach cars and campsites looking for food. But visitor beware—these beauties can be dangerous. They have been known to kick and bite for no apparent reason.

My most spectacular pony sighting was a beautiful group of three, a stal-

lion and two females, standing atop a grassy dune. The horses stood motionless for a long time. They didn't seem disturbed by people strolling on the beach not far below them. These little horses move slowly and radiate a sense of calm. This is a difficult environment for them: the food is poor, the drinking water is salty, the climate is harsh. In the summer, biting insects are so vicious that, to avoid them, the ponies spend much of their day standing in the soothing surf. Still, this is their domain, and the ponies of Assateague meet the challenges with quiet dignity. The National Park Service cares for the ponies and administers the area as a national seashore.

*White snake
with feathers
dancing in the trees.*

At the Chincoteague Refuge, paralleling the road that leads to the main ocean beach, a freshwater channel is home to dozens of great egrets. These tall birds wade into the water, stand motionless, and pluck out fish, frogs, snakes, and other prey with amazing accuracy. With its brilliant white feathers, the egret makes no pretense at camouflage, unlike a nearby heron that is nearly invisible as it lurks patiently in the shadows. Several egrets sunned themselves in trees beside the channel, two engaging in lengthy social behavior before flying away.

The Chincoteague National Wildlife Refuge was founded in 1943, originally in an attempt to save the snow goose from extinction. The refuge has created several vast shallow wading areas to provide an attractive habitat for aquatic birds. Today the refuge's midwinter snow goose population is about ten thousand. For bird-watchers, Chincoteague is a wonder to behold. Spending an hour observing the activity of these geese as they wade back and forth in the shallow water, stroll the sandbars, then take off and land, is like watching an unstoppable force of nature. Congratulations are due to the refuge for rescuing these beautiful birds from extinction.

*Don't look at me
woodland beggar.
Tonight the ocean speaks
my name.*

Deer, the scourge of countless suburban backyards, are well represented at Chincoteague National Wildlife Refuge. There are two varieties of deer, though one of them is classified as a small elk. Shown here is the Virginia white-tailed deer. The other species is the Japanese sika, which was introduced to the refuge many years ago and has prospered.

I photographed the deer opposite while I was driving on the three-and-one-half-mile Wildlife Nature Loop late one autumn afternoon. This a magnificent experience and explains why Chincoteague is one of the most visited national wildlife refuges in the country. Because the landscape inside the looping road was dry when I visited, comparison with the Serengeti Plain was inevitable.

Chincoteague is also home to another herd of wild ponies, kept separate from the northern herd and numbering about one hundred and fifty. The southern herd is more difficult to spot, spending much of its time in distant marshland. This herd is actually owned by the Chincoteague Town Volunteer Fire Department, and every year the volunteers round up the horses and swim them to Chincoteague Island.

*Blade of grass
be strong
as you confound
your mighty foes.*

You may ask, what does all this attention to salt marshes and wildlife have to do with beaches? When it comes to Assateague Island, the answer is everything. Without the living

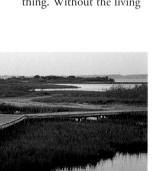

anchor of woodland, cordgrass, and phragmites, the barrier island would dry up and blow away.

Although Assateague is very narrow, it contains several distinct and interconnected environments. They are the sandy beach, the dunes, a desertlike area just beyond the dunes, woodland thickets, tall pines, and salt marshes. A visitor to Assateague can cross all the zones in short order, but a quiet and mindful walk will expand an understanding of the fragility of the total beach environment.

The birth of the salt marshes is intimately connected to the beach and the ocean. In times of great storms, surging waves overflow the island and deposit vast quantities of sand and salt water on the leeward side. Eventually these relatively protected sandbars create a stable area of sea grass and calm water. These salt marshes soon harbor and produce life at an astounding rate. They also help prevent the island from being pushed toward the mainland by the force of the surging ocean.

The Hamptons

Not far from New York City are some of the most perfect beaches this side of the Caribbean. The white sandy beaches of Long Island's South Shore extend about a hundred miles, from the city limits to the Montauk Point Lighthouse. The reigning capital of this blissful treasure coast is the Hamptons, a cluster of charming towns on Long Island's East End.

No flowers here,
it is the sun
that blooms
from the yellow sea.

I was on Atlantic Beach just outside of Amagansett. I was late, it was 6:45 a.m., and I had missed that ethereal glow that occurs just before sunrise.

Even so, the morning was fine, and I was nearly the only person on the beach. I was enjoying that solitude; how glorious and refreshing to escape from the world. A tropical storm had passed through, hundreds of miles to the south, on the night before, and the surf was like a wall of water. The breaking waves came in at six-second intervals. Standing here at the western boundary of Hither Hills State Park, I had arrived at my soul's destination.

Writers of pop psychology books suggest that we all create a safe haven in our imagination, a place to which we can withdraw and be nourished when things get tough. For years, this had been my interior safe haven, and here I was, home at last.

butterfly on the beach

There are unexpected moments on the beach that can't be shown in a photograph. As I continued my stroll on the beach at Amagansett, a monarch butterfly appeared. It fluttered from one flowering dune plant to another. Then it flew higher, leaving the dunes completely behind, and headed toward the waves crashing onto the beach. As I hurried after the now distant butterfly, I wondered what could justify such behavior.

Soon another fluttering monarch appeared from out of nowhere and approached the original butterfly. They came closer together, circled one another as if dancing in the air, then proceeded together down the beach. Later in the day, I saw great groups of monarchs in Amagansett and Montauk. It seemed as though there were millions.

Walk slowly, look closely, and witness the countless other small wonders of the world. Some of the best parts of the beach are experienced just a short distance from the shoreline, such as these phragmites glowing in the sun.

looking at the waves

Hearing
my breathing,
with half-closed eyes
I see the ocean.

It's not easy to leave the beach at the end of the day. Wouldn't it be wonderful to stay a little longer; just a few more minutes to better remember this glorious perfection. It would be lovely to keep that peaceful feeling alive and allow the waters to wash away the distractions that plague us. If we stay long enough, I feel certain that some kind of dormant ability to see clearly and with kindness will be awakened.

But it's time to leave. We can promise to remember the surf pounding the sandy beach on a sunny day, with all the power of a vast ocean behind those waves. And some quiet day we can listen to the slow steady beating of our own hearts and know that we have heard the ocean again.

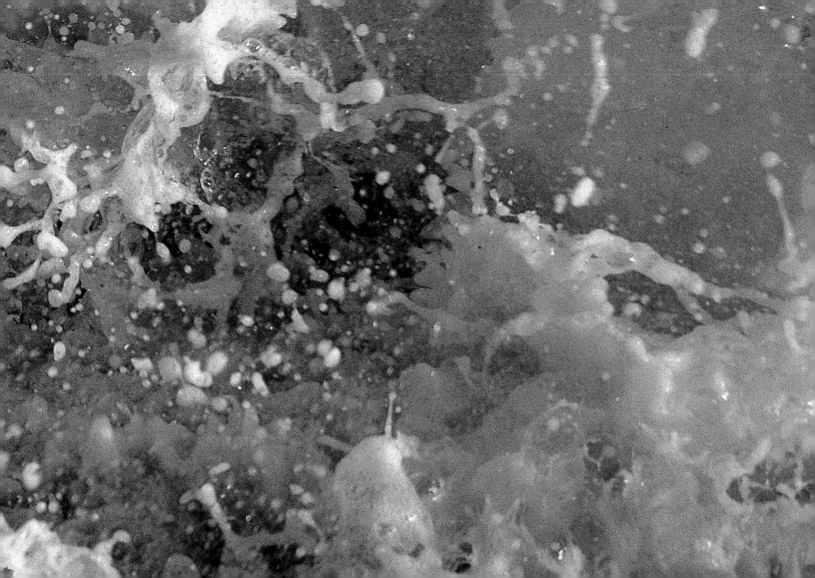

young fishermen

As I walked along the beach, the private houses lining it seemed to me not luxurious, but rather a little institutional. The biggest beach houses have a demeanor of inviolable fiefdoms—fenced, walled, and unfriendly.

Then figures stepped from the shadows into the long fingers of sunlight that still illuminated the beach. They were just there to absorb the moment as it turned a misty orange. Two laughing young men appeared, tried their hand at surf casting, and eventually left, still laughing.

*A sea
of grass also,
no ships yet plow
through your waves.*

Everyone has their own schedule and people love the thrill and fun of the Hamptons beach at midday. But if I have the luxury of time, I use the late morning and early afternoon as an opportunity to poke around the neighborhood and do a little exploring and discovery. Let others soak up the noontime rays of the sun, I say. I prefer a pleasant lunch at Candy Kitchen in Bridgehampton.

As the afternoon progresses, I return to the sea, and as all the world becomes aglow, I savor the special beauty of the beach.

*What pains
someone took
to make this place.
Let me linger.*

We are so lucky to have the hundred miles of lovely sandy beach on the South Shore of Long Island. New Yorkers may take this well-preserved

and well-maintained beach for granted, but it is hard to believe that such a beautiful place can be surpassed. New Yorkers are also fortunate that the shoreline has retained its great sweeping panorama. The high-rise condos that dominate the landscape of other beaches are absent here. Walking on the beach at Bridgehampton, the only vertical objects in sight are a stick planted in the sand and tall waving stalks of beach grass. Long may they wave.

*Mountains
in the sky,
I looked away.
Now here you are.*

I think it must have been the heavy clouds moving in from the west that made this particular sunset so memorable. We stood on the beach for an hour, stunned by the evolving and intricate display surrounding us. Each quadrant of the sky was putting on its own show. Orange and gray to our backs, pink and magenta to the west, and when I looked to the east, I was overwhelmed by the mountains of gray and purple clouds above the beach.

We felt privileged to witness such an incredible sunset, and I wondered how often sunsets in the Hamptons are so incredible. Back in the city, later in the week, I described that evening to a friend, who from childhood had spent most weekends on the East End of Long Island. He had also been there that evening and couldn't remember in all his years a more spectacular display.

Moon
constant companion,
walk with me
into the dusk.

After the sun was below the horizon and the fireworks appeared to be over, we headed back to the parking lot, walking slowly on the soft, deep sand. I stopped and looked back one last time, not expecting to see the subtle scene that had developed. With the sun gone, the air was suddenly cooler, and fog was forming above the beach. Surprisingly, there was still some color left in the sky. But now the full moon glowed through the light veil of mist, presiding over the deepening twilight.

Montauk Point is twenty miles down the road from East Hampton, and it has its share of fancy beach houses, like the Hamptons. However, instead of a lifestyle, Montauk has a lighthouse.

During the nineteenth century, Montauk was either a traveler's last view of land before reaching the British Isles or the welcome first sight of America to immigrants. Until the Statue of Liberty was erected, the Montauk Point Lighthouse had that same patriotic appeal.

The lighthouse was built in 1796 on the orders of George Washington, to encourage American commerce by preventing the loss of ships and trade. Building the lighthouse in a desolate spot was an ambitious undertaking. But it was built for the ages, with sandstone walls, at the bottom level, that are six feet thick. It is one of the few American lighthouses of that era that still stands.

*Purple sea
at twilight,
tell your children
they have guests.*

That noontime, as I was leaving the Montauk Point Lighthouse, all the vehicles in the parking lot should have been a clue. Though I read the sign at the gate that said "Surf Casting Capital of the World," I didn't realize what was going on until I returned that same evening.

I was simply looking forward to a quiet twilight walk. When I descended the steep trail down to the beach, I saw hundreds of surf casters lining the shore. Every rock for as far as the eye could see had a fisherman standing on it. Then I remembered . . . it's late September and the "blues are running." Though it looked like some kind of fantastic twilight ritual, I had come upon participants in the following day's Bluefish and Striped Bass Surf Fishing Tournament.

Block Island is a place apart. For many years, this New England island did not receive the attention lavished on its sister islands, Nantucket and Martha's Vineyard. But at last Block Island has been recognized as "one of the last great places in the Northern Hemisphere." It is rugged and unspoiled, with a rolling rural landscape that seems like a chunk of Ireland placed off our own shores. Here we see the island as it was a few years ago, but having a keen sense of preservation, Block Island will always remain the same.

Between
the fence posts
behold the world
of light.

Seen from distant Montauk Point, Block Island is a hazy low rectangle on the horizon. The one-hundred-and-fifty-foot-high bluffs rising from sandy beaches give the island its solid appearance. That appearance would seem to be the origin of the name Block Island. But, in fact, it was a Dutch explorer, Adrian Block, who saw the island in 1614 and bestowed his own name upon it.

Agricultural for most of its history, the invention of the passenger steamboat in the nineteenth century made Block Island accessible to vacationers from "America," as old timers used to call the mainland. Great wooden hotels were built for the tourist trade, but in the twentieth century an even newer technology, the automobile, made most of the hotels obsolete.

Block Island was forgotten for a while but it endured, and a few hotels remain.

an island of ponds

Block Island measures seven miles long and three miles wide, with seventeen miles of beach coastline. Though small, the island has a remarkable three hundred and sixty-five freshwater ponds. That is clear evidence of Block Island's geological origins, in that period of great change, the Ice Age.

Twelve thousand years ago, as the glaciers retreated, the islands south of New England were created from the vast amount of rock and sand that the

glaciers had left behind. That material is called the glacial moraine. On the landform that would one day be Block Island, many chunks of soil had been scraped out by the glaciers and great blocks of ice were left behind. The ice eventually melted, and Block Island's numerous ponds were created.

the white boat

Sea of azure blue,
where do you go?
Come and
play with me now.

Perhaps more egalitarian than some of its neighbors, Block Island has no private beaches. The shoreline is unspoiled and open to all. While many beaches are remote and secluded, Town Beach, shown here, is in the thick of village life. The boat on the beach is a surfboat used by lifeguards. Just out of the picture is a passenger ferry, arriving from Point Judith, Rhode Island.

90

Homecoming vessel,
splendid in the sun,
just a smile and
your journey is done.

Part of the mystique and fun of Block Island is taking the short ocean voyage necessary to get there. The crossing is only twelve miles, but that's long enough to enjoy the sea breezes with a hot cup of coffee in hand.

Watching a ferry arrive is almost as much fun as arriving on one. It's fascinating to follow the incoming vessel as it inches its way across the horizon. The eventual arrival of the afternoon ferry brings a mild surge of excitement to the relaxed inhabitants and vacationers already on the island. Examining the passengers as they disembark is a most refined and acceptable kind of people watching. Who knows? You might actually be there to meet someone. If not, well, there's always the next ferry.

*The wind has
left his shadow
in the sand.
I stand and wait.*

A walk on the beach is an act of participation with the natural world, a kind of collaboration. There are endless small negotiations to conduct. For example, splash in or avoid the incoming surf, put on your sandals, take off your sandals . . . and so forth. If walking in the city required so many minor but time-consuming readjusments, it would take an entire day to buy a quart of milk. But of course, that is really the fun of being on the beach.

Without much effort, the elements can put an unprepared visitor to the test. Consider a brisk late afternoon breeze blowing sheets of sand across the beach. To begin with, it's painful. You can't see, sand is everywhere—in your mouth, in your hair.

You'll be lucky if your camera ever works again. However, one beautiful result of wind on the beach is the creation of sand ripples and the trailing tails of sand behind pebbles—the wind shadows.

A good time to wander is after the afternoon ferry has gone back to the main-land. Town Beach, though lovely, is small and is soon explored, and other desti-nations beckon. This is a good time for walking out of town, past white wooden houses and his-toric hotels, over rolling hills, toward another view of the surrounding ocean.

Looked at from a new perspective, it's clear how separate and self-contained Block Island is.

Caught in the glow,
stop evening
before moving on.

Living by the ocean is not easy. An island in the North Atlantic is subject to vast and constant extremes of weather, heat, humidity, hurricanes, and isolation, which all put strain on the human ability to make a home and create a community. Block Island's resources are limited in an economic sense, but it is rich in beauty and in the excitement of living on the edge.

The Oregon Coast

Walking the Oregon coast is a wondrous geologic adventure. The shoreline is rugged, with steep cliffs and wide sandy beaches, as well as huge stone monoliths, called sea stacks, jutting from the water. This is not a placid landscape, but it is far from forbidding. It is stunningly beautiful in a fantastic and wild sort of way. Because the state of Oregon administers nearly the entire coastline, beachwalkers can enjoy miles of unrestricted freedom unlike anywhere else.

*On the beach
an ancient mountain
stands.
Did I hear a seabird
cry with joy?*

The coast of Oregon is a dramatic place, but Haystack Rock at Cannon Beach provides a drama all its own. Created by intense volcanic activity, the Haystack stands at two hundred and thirty-five feet and is the third largest marine monolith in the world.

It dominates the wide beach and reminds me of a small planet fallen to earth intact, with all its exotic wildlife still in place. The Haystack teems with life.

Thousands of birds nest there, and each species has its own niche. At the top of the rock lives the tufted puffin, the seabird with the striking white, black, and orange face. Puffins nest in dirt burrows they dig to protect their precious single egg. On their

first flight, baby puffins hurl themselves from cliffs, trusting the distance will give them the speed they need to fly.

in the tidal pool

The other great natural habitat at Haystack Rock is the tidal pools. Seen here, the black volcanic basalt rock, with its attached barnacles, is exposed at low tide. This is a dangerous time for living creatures in tidal pools, since thoughtless visitors can be a major threat. The Haystack Awareness Program is an organization determined to protect this fragile ecosystem. Volunteer marine biologists instruct visitors on good tidal-pool etiquette. The rules are simple: no climbing on the rocks beyond the posted signs, and never touch or collect any living thing. With that in mind, there is still tremendous fun to be had at Haystack Rock. Scrambling around and exploring, beach walkers see an environment that spends half its lifetime under the sea.

Mountain mists depart,
you are still here.
Tomorrow
I will look again.

It was a cannon washing ashore in 1846 that gave Cannon Beach its name. And neighboring Hug Point got its name from the stagecoach trails of the nineteenth century that hugged the rocky shoreline.

Here at the Hug Point promontory, steady pounding by the sea has carved a sea cave from softer rock. Eventually, the expanding cave will totally penetrate the rock and Hug Point will become a sea arch, similar to the many that already grace the Oregon coast.

Weather conditions seem to change hourly here, and the tides can be especially treacherous. They move in fast and can strand unsuspecting visitors. Even as I took this photograph, on the other side of this promontory, after just an instant, my teenage son was surrounded by the incoming tide and had to wade back to the beach through knee-deep water. At least he thought it was fun.

Today
I've walked and walked,
and tomorrow
I will walk again.

The beaches of the Northwest are often littered with trees uprooted by heavy winter storms. Ambitious beachcombers, who have so much free building material, can't resist the urge to create. Puzzling structures, either free-form shelters or just sculptures, are the result. At night, these creative efforts are a good source of kindling for bonfires. Cannon Beach after sunset can be a glowing panorama, with dozens of giant bonfires burning. It's like a gathering of the tribes of some ancient people, camping in the presence of the looming monolith on the beach.

It's hard to resist the countless beautiful stones on the beach. But I would have passed this lovely miniature tower if I hadn't rested for a moment on a tree stump and glanced in its direction.

In these two pictures we have actually left Oregon. This is Dungeness Spit in the state of Washington.

Cedar Key

To experience wild semitropical beaches in the Big Bend country of Central Florida, go to Cedar Key.

Cedar Key is a small fishing village whose commercial glory days ended more than one hundred and twenty years ago. It is located on a small island connected to the mainland by a three-mile causeway. One side of the island faces lovely bayou country; the other side faces the Gulf of Mexico and the many uninhabited islands of the Cedar Key National Wildlife Refuge.

A dewy path
through the morning gold,
hidden sights
I will soon behold.

In the 1860s Cedar Key was a town with great expectations. It was Florida's second largest port, an important railroad destination, and a manufacturing center. Unfortunately for Cedar Key's boosters, the uncertainties of nature and commerce permanently condemned Cedar Key to the status of a historical footnote.

The local cedar forests had been the original source of Cedar Key's wealth. The cedar wood was used to manufacture pencils, and before too long, all the cedar trees had been cut down. To compound the bad news, the growth boom expected as a result of the new railroad never happened. Tampa, not Cedar Key, was designated as the Gulf coast's deepwater port. Finally, tragically, a devastating hurricane in 1896 literally finished the town off.

What's there now are a few old buildings, a fishing pier with a large pelican population, some good motels and places to eat, friendly people, and a beautiful natural environment, including this grassy path leading to the bayous.

end to the long walk

Undoubtedly of more importance to present-day Cedar Key than its defunct industry were the journals of pioneer naturalist John Muir. In 1867 Muir ended his epic walk across America at Cedar Key. Suffering from malaria, he spent some time recovering there and became entranced with the dense tropical forests and the multitude of aquatic birds. When his notes were finally published in book form, Cedar Key was given a chapter, and the area gained prominence for its natural assets.

The name "nature coast" is now used to describe this stretch of Florida's Gulf coast. Miles of state parks, wildlife refuges, and nature preserves provide a much needed sanctuary.

Here and on the previous page are photographs taken in early morning with the mists only recently dispersed. The grassy path leading to the bayou glows in the warm colors of dawn. A few more steps and the still waters are seen, reflecting the soft colors of the calm morning sky.

John Muir described the islands around Cedar Key as green emeralds set into the waters of the Gulf of Mexico. These natural gems are no less enticing today. Isolated and reached only by boat, many of these islands belong to the Cedar Key National Wildlife Refuge. Because some are sanctuary for nesting birds, entire islands may be off-limits to visitors at certain times of the year. And at all times, to protect the fragile ecology of the island's interiors, only the island beaches may be visited.

Atsena Oti is the most accessible of all the islands. It was the location of much local industry in the nineteenth century, and Atsena is still privately owned. Now it is possible to take a limited tour into the island and see relics of the past. Despite its history, while approaching the island by boat, it seems impossible that Atsena was not always the perfect image of a primal paradise. Although scarcely a mile boat ride from town, Atsena appears as untouched as a remote island in the South Pacific.

Ferryman stop the boat.
Let my heart
name this unknown place.

I was filled with antici-pation as I finally set foot on Atsena Oti. On the previous evening, I had spoken to a local man on the town fishing pier, and he mentioned alligators and swimming rattlesnakes in the area. But the tour-boat company that dropped me off on the island that morning hadn't warned about dangerous wildlife, so perhaps my fears were unwarranted.

As it turned out, I saw no dangerous creatures on Atsena Oti, but rather a fascinating world of dense tropical forest and a beau-tiful little beach. This was a living, working beach, littered with fallen trees, seashells, seaweed, sea grass, and rather coarse sand. Before I could set foot on the beach proper, I needed to carefully pick my way past a barrier of sun-bleached tree stumps.

the unexpected shore

*First one step
and then stop,
walk lightly on the
shards of forgotten days.*

For me, this untouched stretch of sand comes close to encapsulating all the emotions conjured up by the words "a quiet walk on the beach." It was deeply relaxing here, but there was also a sense of discovery and a hint of the unknown.

And I was very much alone. The only fresh footprints on the beach were my own. Rusted iron plates protruded from the hard sand, most likely remnants of a ruined factory building. The warm day and fragrant vegetation enveloped me with a sense of well-being, but there was also the tantalizing thrill of mystery. I had seen many beaches, but this was special. Here was a place that had known the heavy hand of civilization but was now fully returned to its primal state. The sky, sea, and sand were all that mattered. Yet it was enough to nourish my body and soul. Weeks later and thousands of miles away, I would still dream of this place.

Most prominent among the islands of the refuge is Seahorse Key. This key can boast of being west Florida's highest point, having a fifty-two-foot-high sand dune. There is also an important University of Florida marine research station on the island, located near an 1851 lighthouse.

Except for the station, the island is strictly off-limits for much of the springtime. Even boats are not allowed to approach within thirty feet of shore from March through June in order to protect the nesting colonies of herons, egrets, pelicans, and ibis.

of, a plenitude of birds,
vegetation thrives here,
with eastern red cedar, saw
palmetto, Spanish bayonet,
wild olive, and prickly
pear.

More than one hundred
thousand birds are said to
inhabit the island, and it is
one of the largest rookeries
in the South. Huge flocks
of perching birds have
denuded many trees
around Seahorse Key.
Despite, or perhaps because

a place of healing

Cool breezes
ruffle pelican feathers.
Across the water, Atsena,
already deep in night.

On the beach, there is no need to practice meditation or have a glass of wine to relax. The rhythm of the waves will soon calm the shallow, harried breathing of the newly arrived visitor. The frenzy of our complex civilization is washed away and is replaced with a natural joy and zest for life.

The beach is a place of healing. I once knew a doctor who prescribed a week of restorative relaxation at a warm tropical beach as a sure remedy for health problems medicine had difficulty curing. He wasn't certain where the curative powers resided; in the salt spray, or the pure air, or the sun, or a combination of them all. But he had seen the beach cure his patients again and again.

While walking on a beautiful beach we move in step with nature's most basic music: the song of the earth and the moon. The tides, the months, the cycles of our lives are all part of that healing song.

Although I have left Atsena Oti behind, I intend to continue listening to that primal music as I walk on other beaches.